Introduction

A charge frequently levelled against psychoanalytic practice is that it is exclusive, intellectual and elitist. It is therefore a shame that many analysts, when they do 'present' in public, tend to read out a paper and in so doing kill dead the enjoyment of their rich content. While privileging clinical excellence is vital, as is standing firm in the face of the tumult analytic thinking inherently evokes, making psychoanalytic ideas more broadly accessible does not have to equate to levity or compromise. We tend to speak about *what* we do rather than *how* we do it. The challenge is to find a way to speak out differently.

In the current regulatory climate, the pressure within statutory services is to provide increasingly short term, solution-focussed work, where goals are agreed with the client at the outset, and perhaps even before the full nature of the 'presenting problem' has been established. Implicitly and sometimes explicitly, the primary aim is to get as many people back to work, and as quickly, as possible. GPs are directing their patients towards computer programmes and wellbeing websites, while counsellors and therapists in the public sector are finding themselves required to fill in standardised forms and questionnaires with their clients in every session. All in the name of evidence based practice.

Thus, the available time and space in which a person can express and come to understand themselves and their difficulties gets reduced.

There is more reason now than ever to convey the awesome beauty and potency of analytic ideas about the human condition. Psychoanalytic thinking has by its very nature always been disquieting and challenging: it stirs us up and, by shedding light on our established assumptions, makes us available to new ways of thinking and being. Freud's own paper "The Resistances to Psychoanalysis"[i], in which he explains deftly how and why it is not an easy subject to introduce to people, remains as relevant today as when it was written in 1924. On the other hand, the proliferation of the counselling and therapy 'industry' has brought a popularisation of 'soft' notions like 'getting closure', 'positive thinking' and the expectation that happiness can and should be universal. This has resulted in a feminisation of the public reputation of the field, which lays us open to easy ridicule, if not outright attack. I do not think it is mere fantasy that there was a time when the 'talking cure' commanded more respect and held authority in both the intellectual and clinical challenge it presented – at least therapy was seen as scary and difficult rather than as self-indulgent. And it was intellectually interesting beyond its own compass, influencing artists, playwrights, authors and auto-biographers. It was understood that analytic work was neither comfortable nor complacent.

To my mind, the current State bid to regulate the talking therapies is *inter alia* a reaction to this feminisation of the public persona of therapy in the face of which we need to come clean about how hard and painful a potent psychoanalytic process is. Burgeoning simplifications of attachment theory and the over-privileging of 'the maternal', notions of nurture, empathy, 'containment' and 'relationship' set against denial of the negative transference and of the power of the unconscious have emasculated the field – "it is rather like catching a tiger and saying "nice pussy cat" as Wilfred Bion put it.[ii] We need to get clearer again about where we stand – which is in a place of difference. It's time to answer back and to state our position, our identity and face our differences, between the

For

Eric Pomet & Grisélidis Réal
who taught me the importance of courage in the external world
&
Nina Farhi
who taught me the importance of courage in the internal world

With immense gratitude

many kinds of analytic practice and practitioners, and between analytic practice and everything else. Adult life is tough, and full of challenges and uncomfortable encounters. Consequently there is conflict, so let's get on and face it. Anything to get us out of the cloying, airless nursery.

I want to try to say something about psychoanalytic processes as I have come to understand them. My aim is to counter some popular assumptions while also conveying the gravitas and the contemporary importance of the field. By highlighting the pivotal importance of continually challenging, developing and honing our ways of working and thinking, I will show how psychoanalytic theory and practice can avoid complacency and remain lively, engaged and perhaps more relevant today than ever.

This is going to be an evocative exposition, where I will unashamedly speak from myself. The emerging argument will be accompanied by elements from contemporary and ancient cultural sources, and by open references from my professional and personal experience.

Ruth Jones
June 13th, 2010

Getting going

It has taken time to gather in what I want to say – it wasn't all there in the beginning but has come as felt and thought fragments, threads of enquiry, open minded musings, including some dead ends, which have been collected, teased out, carded, sorted and spun together. Bit by bit my meaning has emerged. It is now a year since I bought a web book thinking I was ready to start writing. And a year it has remained in its box. Of course, stretching a canvas doesn't make a painting appear, picking up a pen doesn't write a poem. That wide-spread symptom of contemporary gadgetry, the Power Point Presentation, certainly doesn't guarantee an interesting talk any more than wool-gathering makes for an interesting paper! And a brass plaque doesn't make a meaningful therapist, any more than turning up session after session makes for a meaningful therapy. So what does?

Precious time / real time /spending time

It is over 2 years since I finished my psychoanalytic training and 8 years since starting it - 10 since beginning to prepare the candidacy requirements. That's a long time and involved a hard-earned investment on many levels. What has it all been for, you may ask. What is it, this human activity where I sit with other people for 50 minutes at a time? 50 minute pieces of the finite amount of time which is my life, whose length I cannot predict, and 50 minutes of theirs, these people whose longevity is equally uncertain. Some are younger, some older. Older age increases both of our awareness of the inevitable limit to the time available - come what may the fifty minutes are spent out of just 10, 20 could it be 30 years remaining, who knows. But youth provides no guarantees – the college student who went to bed and didn't wake, the post doc research scientist who died riding his mountain bike in the Alps – we all know similar stories. Youth is no guarantee, but it does have the ability to sustain the illusion that death is a fact of life we can disregard for a while longer.

So why spend precious amounts of 50 minutes sitting with people, initially strangers, and why do they come? What motivates us? Are they clients? Patients? I prefer the term "people", 'my people' if you must but with an acute awareness that they are not 'my', not mine at all. And yet we may spend some of the most important, most meaningful, most vibrant moments of our lives together, before we eventually go our separate ways, in all likelihood never to meet again.

Being prepared to practice, or is it practise?!

Having trained long and hard to be able to just sit with someone, I also accept the particular working conditions of self-employment (no apparent 'job security', no sick leave or holiday pay) to be able to do it. There is no backup financial support - no family legacy, no other sources of income. I come to it alone. This is part of, but not the whole reason, why I charge for sessions – I have to be paid to be able to do this kind of sitting, otherwise I would have to spend the time doing something else instead to earn a living.

This is an activity to which I feel a commitment like no other - still the same person, the seriousness with which I engage in this professional activity is as I could never have imagined while employed in other capacities. And the seriousness is welcome, it is not a deprivation, I embrace it - it holds me too. It is an adherence, an observance and a practice. Those are all words we also use for a faith, and in some ways there are similarities – both a faith and therapeutic work create places and times for particular kinds of experiencing to become possible. Both provide structures for interrupting the flow of ordinary time with distinct pieces of time set aside for unordinary experiences.

Being serious about this undertaking has meant lifestyle planning and shifts, based on knowing how much of this kind of work is within my capacity. Living within the means of that, while not working more than I can manage, I have found a resting point, a balance where a quantity of work provides a quantity of income which works for me for the time being. This kind of tipping point, this balance, will be different for everyone depending on all kinds of internal and external factors and possibilities. It cannot be facetiously or randomly arrived at, neither can it be imposed by an external authority. It has to have an internal coherence and integrity particular to each analytic therapist in order to create a dynamic tension underpinning the work – the fabric will be corrupted by incoherence, exploitation or levity at this point. So again, somewhat like a faith, this coherence is not negotiable and neither is it predetermined. My commitment is to practice as fully and with as much structural integrity as I am able at any given moment.

It is becoming clear that I expect more of myself than any regulatory body would ever be able to require. I have to inhabit the dynamic tension of the commitment to this task of *being with* another person – to be part of the lived experience, not somehow outside it. This is not about applying a technique or providing a service inside a framework. I don't '*do* psychodynamic' (as is often said) - I *am* psychodynamic. And I don't try to 'leave it all behind at the end of the day' (another oft repeated mantra in some other modalities) as if the work is somehow separate, elsewhere. I expect to be inhabited by this work, to have it in mind, to have dreams and nightmares and fleeting thoughts and sense impressions about it. This personal engagement is not just personal, it is deeply rigorous and structured; this is not about personality and yet the totality of my personhood is my all that I have to offer and all that I have to draw upon. It's a commitment to a particular combination of thinking and feeling and understanding and knowing that I don't know. Opening myself, with all of my experience and knowledge (including theory) and ignorance, all that I know and all that I don't, I am as much as I can be in a 'held open' kind of way. Then I 'sit back' with it all – creating a particular space, both physical and psychological, which is available for the other person.

So here I am 'sitting back' in a 'held open' kind of way, with no agenda other than to be alive and receptive to whatever comes. This is not a question of 'getting personally involved' in a common way. Instead it means a particular kind of open-minded receptiveness to whatever is there, to whatever a person brings and to whatever comes into being between us. This is a commitment to 'truth', to understanding, to authentic enquiry and to genuine research.

When people come, what they get is me being the therapist that I am capable of being at that moment. This is what they pay for.

It's not just personal

Perhaps you are beginning to wonder whether this isn't all a bit self-indulgent? Or maybe it's frustrating, all very well but not answering the question 'what do you actually *do*?'

I ask you to bear with me, as this is important and has far reaching implications. It is much more than just personal; it is beyond charisma and personalities. I started off referring to the charge levelled against psychoanalytic practice that it is exclusive, intellectual – all in the head - and so I am showing you how this is not so. It is a lived experience.

Letting go of the shore, for sure

When applying for my first training, my first professional training after my degree that is, I had a dream which stuck in my waking mind:

> Some children were playing one summer in the rock pools along the edge of a beach. They pursued minnows with their gaudy fishing nets and touched the tentacles of anemone flowers with their fingers to feel them cling and retract. They tried to pull limpets off the rocks.
>
> And then they happened upon a little spider crab which had been hiding inside its camouflage in a water filled crack. They fished it out, and watched as it flailed its plated limbs. They shrieked and squealed at its articulations, half intrigued and half frightened of being nipped by its pincers.
>
> After a while the parents looked to see what their children were up to. They showed some fleeting interest but then told the children to stop being cruel to the poor creature and to come now and play nicely on the beach. So the eldest child threw the spider crab as far as he could into the sea.
>
> There the spider crab was soothed by the rocking

of the waves, back and forth, back and forth, back and forth.

Until, little by little, it became aware of the force of the water, back and forth, back and forth, pushing it back and forth, back and forth, relentless and ever closer to the rocks. There was nothing to grip on to and the little crab, pushed and pulled back and forth, back and forth grew increasingly desperate.

"Please, oh please stop and let me rest" pleaded the spider crab to the sea. "I'm so tired, please let me go. Please stop".

And the sea replied "Oh I so wish I could, little spider crab, really I do. I too long for rest, I wish I could be still but you see, I can't. I can't stop because I am pulled too, pulled back and forth, by the moon".

As it was an application for an art therapy training, I made a painting relating to this dream for my candidacy portfolio. There it stayed, un-interpreted, remembered from time to time. It was part of a long journey away from the world of quick fixes, of answers and solutions, away from the world of power and 'facts', of right and wrong, and away from the sentimentality that oozes in between those pillars of certainty. It was part of the ongoing discovery of the forces of human nature, the nature that is within us and of which we are made, as implicit and essential to us as is the natural environment around us. That nature with which we are woven through and through, upon which we utterly depend and over which we have so precious little control.

Seeing people

I now live and work overlooking a tidal estuary - the view is the reason for calling my work 'The Riverside Practice'. So why is it that people take a long time to notice that my consulting room has one of the most striking views in and of the area, when ordinary visitors to the house spot it straight away? Why isn't it obvious? And not just to one or two, but to almost all who come for therapy? While it is true that people are troubled when they come (being 'in trouble' after all is what brings them initially), they are also functioning to a greater or lesser extent. So why can't they see the view? Neuroscience tells us that our brain is easily deceived – we don't 'know' as much as we thought we did. Experiments show that we can deliberately trick our brain into seeing stuff where it is not and into not seeing what is there. These days, researchers using scanners can anticipate what a person will decide many seconds before they are consciously aware of making a choice themselves.[iii] We could say, "Well that's it then". "End of story". "It's all about chemicals and electrical impulses which we can record and measure in machines". But isn't that rather a dead end?

What does all of that evidence mean for us people? What does it mean to be human and alive and sentient – what does it mean to perceive and feel and think in the way that we do. What is human experience? Freud referred to the illusion of self-knowledge with his assertion that, thanks to the unconscious, 'the Ego is not master in its own house'[iv], while writers, poets, philosophers and artists have been grappling to make sense of this human subjectivity for millennia.

If we fundamentally cannot know, cannot be sure or certain of anything, and only have the vagaries of our perceptions to rely upon, then surely this must mean that nothing has a fixed meaning and cannot be guaranteed to be 'the same' for different people or indeed for the same person at different times. We need look no further than our experience of time. The clock says how many minutes and hours and yet we talk about time 'flying' and 'standing still'. How we experience a piece of time is anything but measured and objective – it can be long or short, can 'slip through our fingers' or 'weigh heavily' on us. Or memory – things ebb and flow in our minds. We forget things, we are reminded of others; some things we do without thinking and we can't get other things out of our heads. And how do we know whether we see the same colours as the next person? We have agreed what name we give to a particular light frequency but we cannot know whether, when I recognise what I have learned to call 'red', I might actually be seeing what you would know as 'blue'. Shared language fixes all our individual experiences with commonly held words. Therefore we have no way to know whether our experiences are the same as another person's – all we can share is the language we have agreed on to refer to things.

So if all human experiencing is fundamentally subjective and fluid, why is it that some people come into therapy? What kind of suffering brings them to the point of seeking help - what does being 'in trouble' mean if we are all so very much at sea in any case? And what is it that one human being can offer another? Perhaps you are wondering something like 'But doesn't that also mean that you too can't know, can't be sure or certain either?' and 'People want help when they're in crisis and you reel them in and keep them coming because they are vulnerable.' What if that is all true? And if it is, why do I do it? Because I am an exploitative charlatan? A trickster and a con artist? I don't recognise myself in that. Or deluded? Is it all a set-up, a hoax? Well if it is, wouldn't that then also mean that all of life itself is a hoax, where nothing is ever really shared and all relationships are just illusory? That feels like another dead end. Except that it doesn't really matter does it? Even if life as we each experience it is all an illusion, a figment of our own imagination, and we really are all 'islands', it's nonetheless the only life we have and the only way of living available to us, so we may as well get on with living it as fully as we can!

Within therapy there is no material exchange, no product for sale as such, although we could say that something is being rented by the 50-minute hour. Again you may ask, what exactly is it that I am charging and being paid for, beyond my time? I will engage with this question in due course.

Time and space continuum

For now, let's get to the basic structures. I practice in a dedicated room, which stays pretty much the same. There is a sofa comfortably long enough for a person to sit or lie down on, some cushions and a throw, a few ornaments and two plants, three pictures. There is a chair for me and a couple of other pieces of furniture. A waste paper basket, a box of tissues and a silent clock. The bathroom is next door, if needed. So there is a physical space, usually quiet, ambient and uninterrupted. Then there is an agreement about the days and times we are going to meet, and because I operate a sliding scale, a decision about a fee which is meaningful and viable for us both.

In my pre-therapy days, I spent good times socialising and more with particle physicists working on experiments across Europe and North America. And if we think of the therapy situation in terms of a metaphor drawing on what has become a popular contemporary icon, the Large Hadron Collider (LHC) at CERN, we have thus far dug the tunnels and access shafts in the ground (that is, lived life, undergone a training including extensive personal therapy, and made preparations for entering into private practice). We have built the supercollider machinery (created the physical therapy space and established fiscal and professional structures). We have switched on the superconducting magnets (time slots have been allocated to a process which will take place repeatedly – the commitment to go ahead and have regular 'collisions' has been made by both of us). Now the LHC also has a vacuum inside its structure and detectors at different points around its circumference with which to observe particle impacts and detect the by-products of those events. So what will the process potentially be inside our therapy infrastructure?

As therapist, I endeavour to provide as uncluttered an environment as possible; not a vacuum but a relatively clear space. You will remember that I am 'sitting back' and 'holding open'. This is complex and multi-facetted however. Just as any scientific enquiry changes what it observes by the very fact of observing, so being in therapy changes the course of a person's life, because, at the very least, they have decided to spend time and resources this way rather than in some other way. And the room is not empty – there are two participants (two poles of interest) in there – a therapist is inevitably part of the therapy situation. I will return to this later but for the time being let us understand that as therapist, I am trying to provide an open arena for the other person to make use of, inhabit and experience in their own terms. Unlike a more usual (social) encounter between two people, I endeavour to create the conditions for the other person to 'go first' and be as free as possible 'to show themselves being themselves'. This way, we both get the chance to see more clearly the form and characteristics of their ways of being, their assumptions, the qualities of their personalities undistorted by the muddle of everyday social interaction and adaptation. We have, so to speak, turned down the volume of background interference to better hear the pitch of the individual personality resonating in relatively empty space. There are no requirements on a person other than to express as best they can whatever it is that they are thinking, feeling and experiencing in that moment. Our participant is relatively free to exercise his or her own nature just as the particles in the vacuum at the core of the LHC are free from interference from the energetic 'demands' of other subatomic and gravitational forces. It soon becomes apparent that 'adapting to suit the circumstances' is what we are used to, and there is the jarring clatter of attempted adaptations as they fall into the space between us – as if the chameleon can't figure out any colour to be other than its own.

The LHC superconducting magnets require enormous supplies of energy to keep the particles in circulation and not tangled up with the walls of the collider. Similarly it is hard work to keep alive the tension in the therapy situation and keep free association, or 'talking without interference' going on. Freud found that even when he exerted his doctor's authority, people couldn't easily sustain free association. His exasperation with them eased somewhat when he realised that he too couldn't do it perfectly either[v] and that free association - just saying whatever comes to mind - is very hard to do! But when we do manage to maintain this open space, the 'pull' of the transference begins to make itself felt.

So what are the 'detectors' in the analytic therapy situation and how do we make sense of what they are observing? And why bother doing any of this at all?

Being seen

There are many dimensions or registers of experiencing at play. To begin with, there is the way that, when we speak something out loud, it 'separates out' and clarifies itself, it stands alone and we can hear it, *really* hear it. It takes on a feeling tone and resonates in a way which can have a very different impact from when it was embedded in its thought form. Ideas and feelings, when expressed in words (and also through expressive silences) can become isolates – they stand or fall by their own sword. Freud's injunction to try to free associate and say whatever comes to mind, no matter how irrelevant, unimportant or unacceptable it may seem, starts to have its coherence here. To speak whatever comes to the fore means we get to hear the contents of our conscious and unconscious mind as they flow, less contaminated than usual by self censoring. This can be a powerful and startling experience in itself (clusters of particles are being emitted into the LHC).

To speak rather than just think our thoughts means hearing ourselves from a different angle. And to free associate in the presence of another means a further dimension: we are seeing and being seen simultaneously.

When working as an art therapist with children with autism and significant developmental delay, I became interested in the capacity for engaging and interacting which gathered over time in the therapy with these disconnected, fragmented youngsters. For these children, there are particular experiences which have to be assimilated before relational living can occur – for instance where there is no notion of time there can be neither order nor sequence. The child survives in a perpetual present moment, with no sense of past or future so that experience cannot be learned from and there is no hope of a different future to aim for. Everything becomes *everything* – there is no space in mind to imagine that their present experience and feelings might stop, change or be modified and mastered in any way. So everything has to be continually survived rather than lived, and there is no internal 'playground' for imagination or relating to any form of self or other. It wasn't always clear whether there was any awareness of the distinction between inside and outside for some of these raw children – it sometimes seemed that there was no way for them to know any difference between what they were doing and what was being done to them. I imagined a ladder of thought structures needed for naming, locating and making sense of what was going on for them, which had to be climbed before any kind of relational and imaginative living could come into being[vi].

With them, my task was one of supporting and fostering their emergent capacity for being in the presence of, and then involved with, another person. This developmental approach started with my efforts to find fragments of possible meaning in their apparently meaningless rituals and behaviours, though remaining aware that at this point these were only my own thoughts, ideas and associations. I tried to communicate my availability and my interest in trying to understand what the child may be feeling or experiencing, while not imposing any ideas nor making any kind of demand upon them to respond or take in my offerings. This seemed like 'floating ideas on the air', making thoughts available while being very careful to keep sufficient distance too, and not be intrusive with these vulnerable, hyper-sensitive individuals. The slightest mis-attunement could send them 'over the edge' into an 'autistic flap'. Bit by bit, a sharing of experience could become possible: something familiar could begin to ebb and flow between us – particular patterns, gestures or rituals could be repeated and developed over time, with new ingredients being introduced by the child and, eventually, sometimes, by me. Within this developmental framework, a cumulative building up of looking, seeing, looking at and watching each other could coalesce. I learned to recognise an increasing capacity in the child for actively 'seeing and being seen'. Over time this could lead to reciprocity, an emerging dialogue of looking and seeing and watching, out of which play, symbolic mark making, forms of speech and representational drawing could get going.[vii]

Dynamic space

Back in our psychoanalytic therapy situation, we have the fact that there are two persons present – the one who has come and the therapist they have come to. The LHC fires bunches of particles in opposite directions while detecting the 'discharge' or fallout when two of the particles impact each other. Here the metaphor may appear to unhook, for our therapist is both an observer and an active participant whereas the machinery of the detector and the colliding particles would seem to be separate entities of different orders. But not necessarily, for this is the frontier of open research, both in physics and in the therapy, where we venture into an exploration of what is currently unknown, where pre-suppositions and pre-formulated theories will be proven or discredited. This is the point at which both fields of exploration become dynamic, moving from the 'real' of the physical into the 'fluidity' of the intersubjective arena. It is where different orders of things intersect.

Here we begin truly to enter into the realm of the human psyche, psyche being that which remains after we remove all that is physical and mental: what being human is made up of beyond 'meat and mechanics'. We are moving into an exploration of the unconscious, where developmental therapeutic work ends and analysis begins. Likewise, at the LHC, engineering finishes and quantum physics begins. The subject under scrutiny becomes the invisible and the irrational: the unconscious for psychoanalytic work, and dark matter and dark energy for contemporary physics. And what physicists are telling us is that over 95% of the universe is made up of that invisible dark matter just as Freud alerted us to the unfathomable reaches of the human unconscious.

Now we are in the arena of not knowing what to expect, not knowing what we will find, with just our hypotheses to go on. We have to have the courage to revise our thoughts and speculations as we venture into this new territory, using our capacity to make new meaning out of what we encounter as we go. The machinery is operational and collisions are happening, so to speak. We are all, analytic therapists and research physicists alike, now on the path of discovery, reaching away from the place of established knowledge. The focus now shifts onto understanding what is occurring, onto detecting, observing and analysing what the 'collisions' are activating and releasing, what is happening during each encounter in the specially constructed therapy 'space'. And again Freud forewarned against the human inevitability of seeing what you expect to see and being blind to what doesn't fit in with a cherished theory or familiar expectation[viii].

The science has moved into the quantum realm where a particle is both a 'thing' and a 'wave' simultaneously. We can no longer rely on observable, linear logic, because we are now beyond ordinarily sensible facts, evidence bases and measurable, predictable outcomes. This is of a different order: quantum principles apply and quantum phenomena operate in many different dimensions. And in our analytic therapy, our focus is now on attending to the ever changing realm of psychodynamic experiencing.

As well as a vacuum inside the LHC, there is also a temperature approaching absolute zero which is where new things begin to happen:

> *In everyday solids, liquids and gases, heat or thermal energy arises from the motion of atoms and molecules as they zing around and bounce off each other. But at very low temperatures, the odd rules of quantum mechanics reign. Molecules don't collide in the conventional sense; instead, their quantum mechanical waves stretch and overlap. When they overlap like this, they sometimes form a so-called Bose-Einstein condensate, in which all the atoms act identically like a single "super-atom"[ix].*

So what does it mean for the therapist also to be two things at once: both an observer and a participant, at one and the same time? In the therapy situation, we have carefully created the optimal conditions for transference to be identifiable and observable. Of course transference is something ordinary, something we all do all the time – it is the inevitable way that we see anything new through the filter of everything we have known; we have no choice but to measure something new with the yardstick of all our accumulated knowledge. We see new things through the lens of our prior experience and in this way we imprison the new - we are prone to 'deciding' that an unfamiliar thing is like something in our accumulated store of previously encountered events. We do this rather than 'asking' openly what it is. The new thing is robbed of its own identity as we impose our own expectations onto it[x]. Thus the therapist can expect to be denied their own freedom to be as they are, as if they are given a mask, a disguise, provided by the other person. From the inside, it is not easy to know what appearance we have been given to wear, what role we have been appointed. We have to figure it out by noticing the impact it is having on the person looking on – are they frightened or excited or happy or hostile towards our new 'appearance'? We can try to understand the difference between how we are seen ordinarily (the 'who we are used to being seen to be') and how we are being seen now. We observe, we notice, we detect the discord – the gap. The extra layer we are being apportioned, the transference 'disguise', becomes the focus of our attention. It is the 'in-between', this new creation, this discrepancy that becomes the object of our study. In a sense there is a new, additional subject in the room with us which we are trying to identify and decipher. For once the disguise, the transference, is revealed, the potency of this imposter is reduced, and we can get back to the task of making a more 'honest' or 'clear sighted' connection with the other person, in this case the therapist.   This process frees us to leave that particular 'bubble' of self-created assumptions and to begin to meet the world as itself, as it really is. The more we are able to take off the masks we have imposed, the more we can discover who we are really dealing with.

Why does this matter, this 'getting clearer', especially in light of what we were saying earlier about things not ever being fixed, not knowable for sure?   Because creating and sustaining an illusion requires mental effort and psychic energy in comparison with a simple encounter with a truth which just *is*. When a transference belief gets clarified, the world becomes a bit more clear, a bit more independent, a bit more multifaceted, a bit more complex and a bit more simply itself. And we get a bit better at just letting it be. In so doing, we make ourselves a bit freer to just *be* too. So we become a bit freer to be separately, truly ourselves in a world which is a bit freer to be delightfully, awfully, separately simply as it is.

This doesn't change what is there to be seen, doesn't make anything 'better'. We are not in the business of making things alright or changing whatever it is that has happened to a person. Everything comes into its own, whatever it is. But in facing our 'truths', by stepping back from our transference convictions, we can begin being a bit more alive to living with immediacy, a bit more awake to life as it is 'without the middle man'. Just think of how it is when you stand up close to a billboard hoarding - you can only see the dots of colour: you have to step back to be able to take in the whole picture. We must all have experienced the feeling of relief when, after quizzing effortfully, trying to decipher an unclear image, it suddenly snaps into focus. Transference doesn't get 'done' once and for all: seeing something clearly now doesn't suddenly mean we can see everything else clearly all the time, or even that we can see that same thing clearly every time we come across it. It's more like those all-over pattern pictures where a 3D image can emerge if we look at it the right way. Seeing it once makes it easier to look for it but is no guarantee you will be able to effortlessly find the contours of the form again. We have to repeat doing it, to get used to the idea and get better at seeing what is happening, better at stopping before deciding what we think. We have to keep on working at it, and some days that's easier than others.

That said, (we are after all in the quantum realm where a particle can be a wave at the same time!) the following metaphor is also pertinent:

> *If you grow up in a house with black and white TV, and, one day, you walk along the High Street and see a colour television in a shop window, it doesn't necessarily mean you can have a colour television at home. However, from now onwards, you will know that films are made in colour.*

All the kinds of looking and ways of seeing that I am describing are about getting a different perspective on things – a third element enters into the equation: a position, from which to observe or think about something rather than being lost in the bare experiencing of it. When we invoke this 'third position', it serves as a platform from which to observe and think about ourselves, about things in themselves and the relationships between. Getting an insight into how transference happens and how wrong we can be in our assumptions, opens up questions in our minds. This kind of 'blind spot mirror' helps us be less sure of ourselves. We begin to see that we often don't notice what is around us because we are so persuaded by our pre-conceived ideas. When we blinker ourselves, we limit our field of vision to what we already *think* rather than exploring the full scope of what is actually there to be found.

So far, this discussion has been predominantly in terms of how we see things, and what it means to begin to see things differently. However, as when approaching absolute zero, our therapy space is multidimensional and many things can be going on at the same time, in different registers, on different levels. Just as math describes many possible dimensions beyond the four (time-space) we ordinarily experience, there are many mechanisms and structures in the human psyche and many ways of creating and conveying emotional states. The realm of the unconscious is not just apprehended visually and mentally. There are all the different *'shoals of psychic life that swim beneath the analytic dialogue in every session'*[xi]

Hence our psychoanalytic therapy space becomes a living microcosm within which all kinds of things might be going on simultaneously, and where things can 'stretch and overlap' too. Our therapist's job now is to be as alert and attuned, receptive, to as many of them as possible using every aspect of their own capacity to experience. Their body can feel the impact of the other, in the form of physical reactions or somatic sensations – unbearable 'matchstick eyes' in the face of unacknowledged aggression is one of my own stock-in-trade 'detectors'. There can be sense impressions, fleeting thoughts, associations and recollections in mind ('butterfly thoughts' as Marion Milner called them[xii]). There can be an awareness of being pushed and pulled out of shape, being blamed, refused, resented, hated, dumped on, loved and demanded of to be some thing or another, as we are bombarded with projections and dissociated mental contents. There can be 'glass walls of the mind' to crash into when denial and resistances are active and when we reach the edges of what someone can think about – the end of their, or our own, compass. There can be the feeling of being driven mad or seduced, put on a pedestal or denigrated, idealised or felt to be useless, paralysed or paralysing, too clever or too good. Our therapist, if they are to remain true to the 'sitting back' and 'holding open' stance of psychoanalytic work, has no option but to try to draw on their own 'psychic apparatus' to detect and make sense of the impacts and forces being exerted by the psychic apparatus of the other. Like the Bose-Einstein condensate, in this analytic arena something new (a 'super-atom') has been created out of two psyches converging in an 'intersubjective analytic third'[xiii]. Something new has been created which is both to do with and distinct from the two participants – a new entity in between has been created by the interaction of both. (I have always disliked the popular phrase "my other half" – how can this be right? It means that together there is just the one of us. I prefer the idea that my partner and I are two people creating and sustaining something more than the sum of the two of us, which is our relationship.)

Freud long ago said you can't know about or make judgements about psychoanalysis without experiencing it[xiv]. He was also sure that science would eventually demonstrate the validity of his theories. Today neuroscience is beginning to show unconscious processes in action, and 'prove' with scans and neural imaging how one person's mind can have a tangible, measurable impact on another's. Which of course also confirms that we rub off on each other and so need to be careful who we mix with!

One, two, three and more

This is not just a one way street. For the purposes of a psychoanalytic therapy process, there has been an agreement that one person is in treatment and the other is not, at that time. It is agreed that one person, the therapist will concentrate their efforts on being a barometer and receptor for the psychic activity of the other. But one person cannot ever be completely impervious to another, and both get changed through this exposure to a process which includes sustained psychic 'mixing up'. Inevitably the therapist is going to become a bit more like the person who comes, and the person is going to become a bit more like the therapist through a simple process of spending a lot of time in open, close proximity. This is not at all the same as the therapist purposefully exerting influence or exploiting the power of suggestion. Both could never utter a word and it would still happen, and perhaps all the more so for the silence. It is a more concentrated version of something that just happens between people all the time. Jung produced a beautifully simple diagram to illustrate this, where he locates the conscious and unconscious of both people at the corners of a square, and shows how each person's own conscious and unconscious interact, while both people are also interacting consciously and unconsciously with each other, and each conscious

29

is interacting with the other's unconscious *(to look at, it's just a square crossed through from corner to corner).* This is a way to say that a therapist, no matter how far they 'sit back' and how wide they 'hold open', cannot ever simply be a blank, reflecting surface. They will always be a participant, involved in the 'real', material relationship too.

So we can begin to see that it is important to choose your therapist well, and be sure that they are someone you are happy to get mixed up with. We can also begin to see why a piece of paper, a certificate issued by some registration body or another, doesn't provide any assurances or make that decision for us. Perhaps it has the opposite effect in fact – by persuading us that something is certificated by an external regulator, it distracts us from exercising our capacity to take care and be discerning on our own account. Surely it has to be a question of personal freedom and individual choice, and therefore also a question of personal responsibility and inevitable individuality (and I no longer need to point out the paradox inherent in that statement!)

The transference, the 'real' relationship, unconscious processes and intersubjectivity are all at play all at the same time in our dynamic therapy situation. We are experiencing the present, 'here and now' conditions mixed up with the past, where a person is being themselves and who they used to be (in fact or fantasy), while the other is being themselves and being made into someone else, at the same time, and where 'reality' therefore means different things at once. Different registers of experiencing and meaning are coinciding and interweaving constantly. Words can mean both what they say and something else. Images can be descriptions and evocations and disguises and decoys too. An account or a dream can be both accurate and illusory; something can both be itself and stand for something else. The goal, if any, is to bring to awareness this multidimensional unconscious activity and content.

Science is looking to understand the invisible dark matter and dark energy which is thought to constitute so much of the universe, while psychoanalytic exploration aims to plumb the unfathomable depths of the human psyche and understand the workings and contents of the unconscious. Our analytic method (which I have called one person 'sitting back' and 'holding open' for another) is the best detector available to us at this point. With it we are able to fish at least into the surface levels of the unconscious and gather glimpses of repressed, projected, introjected or emerging material. In the consulting room, like in the science situation, we can't seize hold of the psyche but we can glimpse the traces of its presence – always on the move, at one remove. The LHC detector can't 'catch' the content of the crashed particles but it can record impressions of its passing – the graze of its wings as it flies by. We can't study the flight pattern of a butterfly by pinning it to a board. Freud taught us that in dream analysis we are to examine the manifest dream for the latent content, for that lived and felt experiencing which is concealed behind the apparent 'story' and which is only accessible by free associating to the dream material[xv]. Particle physics has undergone a sea-change in the past decades and now researches in a spirit of enquiry predicated on 'not knowing' what it will find. There is an excited anticipation that bodies of theory are equally likely to be disproved or proved. Likewise as a psychoanalytic therapist, we can't 'know', can't be sure of what we will find or where we will need to go with any person who comes to engage in a therapy process with us. We bring our free floating attention with which to meet their free association, and all our intellectual, sensory, psychic and somatic receptors and processors as well. Thus, it is essential to practise freely if our therapist is to be able to work at 'full capacity' and detect the elemental movements in the dynamic therapy: to sense the tug on the line from the other, think associatively and metaphorically, and draw usefully on their associations and sense impressions. The therapist needs to be able to rely on their 'unthought knowns'[xvi] to navigate these uncharted waters of psychic experiencing.

In the finding and facing of what is there to be found, there can be a great deal of pain and distress – after all, we have buried things away and we resist unearthing them again because we, quite ordinarily, want to keep uncomfortable, distressing, discordant feelings at bay. If, as therapists, we are to be free to produce the conditions required for a person to really encounter their 'home truths', we have to be able to withstand the raging of their resistances. To weather the storms and pave the way for a person to painfully step through into their own reality - thus to feel increasingly 'true' to themselves and coherently 'real' as a person - a psychoanalytic practitioner has to be able to make their own decisions about what to say and what not, how to be and how not, and must be freed from the notion of 'mistakes'. This is the realm of exploration and discovery – we have to be able to learn as we go. If there is a constant demand to 'get it right' with a concomitant threat of malpractice suits, it will become like trying to explore the rain forest in a straight jacket – limiting and disabling. The free range hen will be confined to the battery farm, and our tiger will be forced to ape 'a nice pussy cat'. We will be reduced to sticking to pre-determined (so-called) certainties, following well worn (neural) pathways and 'playing it safe' with a primary preoccupation of covering our own backs. Wouldn't this rapidly become the territory of manipulation – shoe-horning people into pre-agreed corridors -

herding - social engineering[xvii]?

On the other hand, what is to say that our therapist isn't actually an exploitative charlatan, making it all up in a void with no rhyme or reason, just throwing out meaningless speculations. Or worse, a sadist who loves making people suffer psychic pain for no good outcome other than their own perverse pleasure? Doesn't this mean that engaging in psychoanalytic therapy is a pretty risky business if there really are no guarantees, no way really to know who is a 'good' therapist or indeed what is 'good' therapy? How can it be alright if there are no predetermined goals? If it is painful and upsetting and a long, hard struggle? Surely it cannot be completely random, can it?

Can it??

I think that there are essential ingredients which do make all the difference. I have alluded already to a complex combination of highly individual factors which cumulate into a 'tipping point' for each analytic therapist, which must be inherently woven through the fabric of every therapeutic structure if integrity is to reign. In looking for ways to articulate the character of this core governing principle which is also a dynamic force in analytic work, I parted company with particle physics. It may well be that this 'partnership in metaphor' could have continued but I didn't want to get overly distracted from my own field by being drawn into studying someone else's subject area. Having enjoyed being able to invoke this third element to illuminate some of my thinking, I am not about to change nature and become a physicist! Indeed this is as it is in psychoanalytic therapy – a person makes use of the therapist to get a perspective on their own conscious/unconscious intercourse so as to better know themselves. The purpose is not to change into being a different person just as my point here is not to adopt a different profession. We all remain who we are – it is our understanding of who and what that is which changes, that is all.

Kavannah

Casting the net wide and, although not Jewish myself, I came across the notion of 'kavannah' in Jewish mystical theology which seems to articulate something close to my meaning from here on.

The term 'kavannah' has evolved and changed considerably over very many centuries, as has the spelling. These changes run in a similar vein to the development of my own thinking as a therapist. I now believe that the decisive component in any meaningful therapy is that the process of change and 'becoming more fully alive to ones own living' must be conducted with a broad commitment and active rigour conducive with the principles encompassed in this concept of kavannah. I would also assert that if there is any influence to be transmitted by the therapist to the other person, it can and must only be in the spirit of this uniquely individual commitment.

Once again this is not a simple, static idea. Kavannah initially referred to an attitude of 'intention' and 'awareness of what one was doing' in relation to prayer, which included 'reflection on the meaning of the words'. In the Middle Ages it was declared that *"Prayer without* kavvanah *is like a body without a soul or a husk without a kernel"*[xviii]. The parallels with setting out on the therapeutic project are clear.

Over time, the Kabbalists developed this idea of an attitude or approach by bringing a new dimension of abstraction to bear: a human 'intention' expanded to encompass 'liturgical intentions'. The significance was no longer simply in the meaning of the prayer words *per se*, but in the words as clusters of letters where the letters themselves evoked divine associations. Therefore the attitude of kavannah became a multi-layered engagement with the meanings behind the words in addition to their 'face value', linking through the component letters as signifiers of divine concepts. Like Freud's unconscious, the important meaning is behind or beneath the surface word or image, contained within it but in a different register. Hence, true prayerfulness, like psychoanalytic work, required concentration on these deeper, 'hidden' levels, and prayer was understood as helping to re-establish the 'flow of grace'. This links with the move from developmentally-based therapy into the realm of seeking out and grappling with unconscious meanings in order to release 'damned up'[1] psychic contents.

The definition of kavannah continued to evolve. The Hasidim developed this idea of codified meaning within the prayer's words and letters into something more akin to 'pushing through' in contemplative prayer, with the aim of reaching beyond the worldly to meet in communion with God. Praying thus became an emotional and enthusiastic act, where it was the emotional pursuit that mattered. In the sense that there was now the potential for a meeting or joining with God, a relationship of sorts, we can see parallels with psychological notions of attachment and object relationship. Prayer also now serves as a vehicle for breaking out of nature towards the spirit, just as psychodynamic work aims to get past the material world of cognitive structures, somatic symptoms and emotional blocks.

---

[1] This typing 'mistake' so beautifully illustrates my point!

This is a tricky business, on several levels. As a system of belief, there is surely a danger of omnipotence in the notion that man can 'meet' God, and a concurrent risk of collapse into magical incantations and delusional theurgy. In the realm of psychology there is the risk of running aground in notions of the relational, and ideas about 'corrective emotional experience'. There can be a fantasy that the therapist can be a new 'nice mummy' who can make it all alright for us and give us a new beginning in a kind of emotional rebirthing. Now of course all new relationships, including the therapy one, bring with them the potential for new experiencing and opening up of different possibilities. But we can't simply erase who we are and how we have become the person we are today who is having these new experiences. There is no magic wand or, to use a Freudian term, we must not avoid the Oedipal drama. Denial is a deadening disconnection[xix]. We have to find our place and our identity in relation to the world – we can't make the world fit in with us and expect to stay sane.

How often do we hear it said that relationships and family, tribe, group, community building and solidarity, bringing children into the world and battling to protect them, giving them as much as we are able, and creating the feeling of safety, entitlement and happiness for ourselves and others, is what makes us human. These are the popularly cited ingredients of a so-called 'life well lived', seen as the most important thing we can do, our best contribution to the present and the future of humanity. It is where we can engage with the best of ourselves and at times the worst too: our humanness. But what happens when we place all of this in a broader context, of globalisation, capitalism and the environmental (un?)sustainability of our treatment of the planet?

Consumption and creativity

The very things we are apt to unthinkingly assume to be the apogee of human social experience also underpin and sustain our oppression of others, both close to home and in faraway or dissociated places. Our modern-day western-world urgency to obtain and consume in order to get more of the things we want for the people we want to please has generated massive over consumption in environmental terms *inter alia*. We long to feel comfortable, safe and satisfied with ourselves, and expect to be free to develop our interests and be creative, all in good conscience. But what does this mean? How can we ignore the cost of our desire for such, oftentimes illusory, pleasures and comforts? Is it not naïve, regressive, aggressive to deny the inevitable price of our consumption which is being paid by someone, somewhere? Surely we know that the gates of the Garden of Eden are closed and that really there is no such thing as a free lunch?! It seems to me that we, in the so-called developed world, are collectively in the depths of Freud's oral and anal stages: we so often behave like the full-of-himself kind of baby who has no regard for the mother and others who both provide the resources he mindlessly demands and who clear up his resultant waste. In this context, if we are the consuming, ruthless, innocent, instinct driven children, where are the adults? We all know how parents, in the middle of the exhaustion of another sleepless night, can feel utterly exploited by the relentless demands of their parasitic infant. Who is carrying the load here? Who is taking care of the bigger picture when our very sense of creative living is currently so bound up with consuming?

First World Capitalism is predicated upon a tyranny of relationship, where family and community bonds are used to uphold systems of inheritance, possession and security. This kind of structure requires split off, forgotten other(s) for its survival – the sweat shop labourers, displaced farmers and urban slum dwellers of the Third World - to fuel the ever consuming, opportunistic capitalism which has been gathering force in the West for decades. This political foray may feel like a shocking excursion into a different register, especially when so many think politics has no relationship with analysis of the unconscious, which after all is amoral and pursues no external purpose. I have brought in this perspective because I want to draw attention to the potential pitfalls of purely relational priorities, in which therapy could become reduced to a kind of glasshouse for reworking early deficits and traumas so we can live more peaceably with ourselves *within* our culture. A way to fit in better and feel at ease. But this is a closed system, self-referential and solipsistic. In a regressed relationship there is always the risk of simply lapsing into comfortable identification (the 'getting stuck in the mother' that Jung warns against[xx]) and recreating ourselves in the image of our therapist, or some idol or other social icon. Collectively we stand on strangers' heads to protect our kith and kin, and our cherished assumptions. Discrimination creates differences with which to distance and displace others: prejudice and proprietorial superiority ensue. It just isn't always as frankly stated as by the Italian Prime Minister 100 years ago, who said "The law is something we apply to our enemies; for our friends we interpret it"[xxi]

The same can happen with professional allegiances and schools of thought, and a therapist, just like anyone else who doesn't keep some sense of connection to the 'external world' on which they depend, is likely to get mired in social engineering or psychological cloning: stuck in the business of producing comfortable fits without asking what it is that is being fitted in with. Familiarity can lead to loyalties, allegiances, dependency and blinkered vision – our comfort can become overly reliant on not rocking the boat or looking too closely. Dissonances and difficulties get smartly silenced or projected. This is potentially the realm of influence, power, discrimination and protectionism as well as love, reproduction, nurture and growth. Now let me be clear: allegiances and relationships are not a problem in and of themselves just as long as we keep them in proportion, and in their place!

Thankfully, there is one more step. Classical Rabbinism saw the danger in this emphasis on Kavannah as a means of meeting God through prayer. In a legend, Baal Shem Tov pronounced a powerful contradiction to the earlier formulation, now saying that *"Prayer* with *kavvanah is like a body without a soul"*xxii because he saw that prayer must be offered up in a spirit of sacrifice. He emphasised that, *"although a man should pray with great attachment to God and with love and fear, he should nevertheless be humble too before God".* In this way kavannah, like everything, has to be thought about carefully, and grappled with as a guiding principle, not a rule or doctrine. Nothing is absolute. Everything can be used, over-used and misused. We can't get too sure of ourselves or too big for our boots – our feet are made of clay. And therefore we will always fail.

Likewise, when we enter into this realm of psychoanalytic work, we need to know that we do not, and must not, have a direct line to God! Proceeding in a spirit of humility, modesty and discretion is vital - there is no place here for pride, self-service or personal ambition. Nor for cowardice and ease and expediency. 'Sitting back' and 'holding open', exploring for the sake of exploring and daring to find what is to be found is our *raison d'être*. A recognition of and accepting submission to this organising principle is our way. If the relational is the realm of analytic frames, this is the realm of governing principles and analytic aesthetics. The female 'space' has to have a 'penis' inside it to be potent[2] otherwise it can collapse into the overwhelming, cloying mother/wicked witch of fairytales and nightmares[xxiii]. And there is no room for the gung-ho: we mustn't imagine for a moment that our tiger is not a tiger! Caution is required in the face of the awesome magnitude, and perils, of this venturing into the unconscious. And these kinds of departures can't be measured or proven. That said, I do believe we know on the occasions when we are in the presence of someone who inhabits the dynamic constellation of tensions I am referring to. To me it feels like being in the presence of deep and ancient times, and brings us in touch with our inheritance, our place in the order of things. We are reminded of what it means to be anchored in the time-honoured lineage of the human race.

Analytic therapy is not in the business of vanquishing a person's history, of overcoming and denying their individual constellation of formative experiences and responses, any more than it is to do with making people fit in (as I said before, fit in to what, after all?) Rather it is to do with accepting and bowing honestly, humbly before each and everyone's own lived and living truth. We are interested in freedom through understanding and acceptance, in liberation not power. We are about submission to the 'what is' for any individual person and not dominion or triumph in external terms. It is neither a crusade nor an occupation attempt. Our purpose is simply enquiry and reflection, and our desire is for exploration. Now, like the man of prayer, it is so easy, indeed inevitable that any therapist will fall short of such exigencies (simplicity is an exactingly tall order), but similarly we have to keep on trying: *"When a man falls from this elevated stage while praying, he should still say the words with as*

---

[2] I am using these terms in their Kleinian analytic sense, as principles, and not in relation to heterosexual genital sexuality.

much concentration as he can muster and he can then try hard to return to his earlier lofty stage[xxiv]".

There are many other practices which engage with this notion of active submission: Islam's recognition of God at the centre of all things, Taoism, some aspects of Buddhism and other Eastern religions which struggle with man's place in relation to universal principles are to name but a few. All are predicated on the idea that there is something bigger than we are, on which we depend and of which we are part. Ecology does likewise.

So what kind of authority can there be in relation to analytic work? I think we can see clearly now why any bureaucratic regulatory body cannot hope to provide any meaningful measure of quality in terms of psychoanalytic therapy. And why and how the installation of any 'evidenced based' regulatory framework will kill off the very practice itself – our free range chicken would be dispatched forthwith to the battery sheds.

What, then, do I propose?

Courageous integrity

Well, 'an active engagement with courageous integrity' is my answer. But what does that mean?

Back to Hasidic theology:

> *"Man's natural existence, subject as it is to pride and to the desire for personal advantage and honour, blocks the path to unification. The life of individuality is in fact a life of plurality, for it derives from nature,*

41

> *whereas the life of the spirit springs from the encounter with the one and only reality, which is the unity of all contradictions and the effacement of all individuality, and as such included, paradoxically, in the divine, 'Nothing'".[xxv]*

Hmmm....

It is important for a therapist who is offering an engagement with unconscious processes to be firmly aware of their place in other registers, including the conscious and material world. Our practice is anchored by a courageous engagement in 'reaching beyond' while also recognising that our individuality includes our mortality and other limitations of the body and of living[xxvi]. We are inevitably implicated in political and social world issues by virtue of inhabiting the planet and being part of a society characterised by globalism and capitalism. And this is courageous because we are doomed to fail: we are utterly of and in our political and social contexts, created within them, belonging to them and so will only ever be able to get glimpses of our specificity at best.

Similarly in the arena of analytic life, theoretical pluralism and its inherent tensions are to be embraced – without them we are at risk of over-privileging one body of theory or school of thought. Wherever and whenever we stake a claim, we are bound to get caught up in proprietorial protectionism to some extent. And after all, theories are just one person's sets of ideas and ways of thinking about things, born out of their individuality, their researches and their experiences. We accept that any collection of analytic thinking has to have an internal coherence to be valuable as a body of theory. But theories may well be at odds or completely incompatible with another set of theory which also has its own internal coherence.

These are the very waters of analytic living, the tense warp and weft of our contemporary project. Engaging with the tensions, with the impossibility of analytic pluralism, is what keeps us abreast of complacency and convenient eclecticism – pluralism does not mean an expedient patchwork of easy ideas but a struggle with multiplicity. (It's like herding cats, be they Schrödinger's or anyone else's!!). We have to inhabit that place of uncertainty in relation to theory, rather than build an encampment on apparently solid and staked out theoretical ground, if we want to minimise our vulnerability to theoretical or ideological self reference or 'ivory tower' disconnection. As therapists of the unconscious, we have to constantly struggle to challenge our core assumptions and battle to be aware of our part in the bigger world picture, be it economic, political, environmental, spiritual or in terms of the range of analytic theory. We have to keep ourselves 'held open' to our specificity, to the particular part we are playing in making collective things happen and then position ourselves actively and courageously in relation to those things. Any compromise tips us over into protectionism and self service again – back into Freudian 'pleasure'. We have to actively engage with our own 'unpleasure' if we are to be 'fit to practise'. It is complacency in this register that makes us unfit. And of course we are bound to fail in this because we are in and of our time and place – it is trying that matters, not succeeding.

Therefore I argue against the long held belief that psychoanalysis and politics have no business together. I disagree. In fact I would say that meaningful engagement with uncomfortable and challenging, social and political responsibility is an essential qualification for ethical practice. Not that any of this should come into the consulting room overtly – let's not forget we are still in the business of 'sitting back' and 'holding open'. What prepares and qualifies us for ethical practice is an active commitment on the part of the person of the therapist to be responsibly engaged, troubled and disrupted by, and therefore not defended against, uncomfortable collective problems of living. This does not mean that analytic therapists have to become activists – we are busy being psychoanalytic practitioners. Indeed, political action can be a way of achieving the very opposite of what I am saying, if it is conducted with a determination to triumph and 'win' – that just takes us back to the pre-Oedipal presumption that we can and should get what we want. What it does mean is that we have to be prepared to face and own our inevitable contribution to collective destructiveness which perpetuates oppression, injustice, inequality, poverty, un-peace and environmental damage. Again, there will be a tipping point involving different factors for different people, so the forms this takes will be different but the principle of active engagement is the universal, unifying and enlivening common factor. It is the commitment to challenging our own specificity and thoughtless comfort. It is the commitment to a position of unrest rather than complacency. In ecological terms it means that the only territory that we can travel into without wreaking further environmental damage is that of the psyche. The human unconscious is the only place we can explore and exploit for resources without degrading the global eco-system on which our lives depend. It is an arena for creativity where we don't simultaneously destroy something of the world as we make something new. It really is the only destination for socially responsible eco-tourism!

I have already said that theoretical pluralism is crucial to establishing this tipping point as any individual body of theory so easily becomes myopic, dulled to its own internal assumptions. In this vein, Jean White eloquently recommends *"For the Lacanians, a consideration of issues of containment and perhaps also more attention to affect may be necessary. For the post-Kleinians, a more serious weighting of external reality, humility and tentativeness, and for the Independents a more robust engagement with human destructiveness could strengthen their praxis"*[xxvii] To this I would add that Jungians beware of dismissing the forces of human aggression and sexuality as Freud's foible. But of course, pluralism is very hard to bear, very uncomfortable, demanding, because inevitably our position is in-between, suspended between the various, deeply contradictory possible ways of thinking. We find ourselves as exiles, dependent on theory but never quite able to settle comfortably with it – always struggling with its limitations and specificities. We are out in the world and can't climb back into the womb, no matter how much we might want to! We stand alone. We have to. We are.

We have to become sea-farers rather than landlubbers! We may as well learn to enjoy the foreshore and grow receptive to its riches with its constantly changing states and moods. It is a place of life, this suspended, simultaneous state of aloneness and utterly dependent involvement.

Hard though it may be to believe, when all these tensions are established and held within the therapist, a great deal of liveliness, playfulness, humour, imagination and fun can be had in the sessions. Change and growth come about, and 'symptoms' abate.

Foreshoring the unconscious

So in response to the question 'what is it that you do?' the answer is 'everything that I am able, and nothing, simultaneously'. I am one of two people in a room, trying to be alive to living; no less, no more. What then happens, what goes on in the therapy, what the substance of the work comes to be depends on what the other person brings to the mix. We go where we go. We end up where we end up. The experience is as it is. We wait and see. Likewise, your response to what is written here will hang on what you bring to it. All I can anticipate is that there will be many, wide ranging reactions depending on who reads this and when and where.

On the foreshore, the water is constantly ebbing and flooding, in and out, always moving, never at rest. This living margin between the land and the sea, subject to the action of the tides, is ceaselessly in the process of becoming dry land or an extension of the sea bed. Always both itself and something else, it is an open subject. Understanding and integration emerge and coalesce through the interaction of a person's unconscious and the terra firma (or at least terra firmer) of the therapist. On the analytic foreshore, psychic states and forms can be experienced and their meanings become accessible through the intermediary of something other. Being available to be something other is what psychoanalytic therapy is and what a psychoanalytic therapist does.

There, I have answered the question for the time being.

But one thing is sure. This is not fixed. Erosion will occur and new silts will be deposited. Over time, I will certainly want to add new elements and alter things I have said. There will be different ways to see some things, I will change my mind about others and stand firmly by still others. This is as it is for now.

And there are other thoughts and ideas that couldn't find a place here, which will have to wait for another opportunity. For as the sea replied to the spider crab

I wish I could be still but you see, I can't. I can't stop because I am pulled too, pulled back and forth, by the moon.

End note

When considering what title to give this little book, I plucked at 'Beachcombing' and 'Walking the Shoreline' before reaching 'Foreshore'. The foreshore is that area of land and water between the ordinary high and low tide marks, a defined area that has belonged to The Crown Estate for centuries. The foreshore is subject to a public right of use but it is permitted neither to trespass on any dry land to access it nor to take anything away from the foreshore.

It was a delight then to find that 'foreshoring' not only pertains to that tidal foreshore but also is a name for supporting and treating wounds where a projectile has gone into and come out of the body. Analytic therapy is inherently to do with sustaining a structure within which it becomes possible to locate,   identify, explore and understand the impact of introjected 'objects' and projected 'psychic contents'. Concurrently, 'foreshoring' holds open the flesh at the entry and exit points, with the purpose of creating the opportunity and conditions for deep healing to take place from the inside out.

References

[i] Freud, S. (1925[1924]) 'The Resistances to Psychoanalysis', in (1993) *Historical and Expository Works on Psychoanalysis, Vol 15,* London: Penguin Freud Library

[ii] These are Bion's words to Hannah Segal when talking about the aims of psychoanalysis which she repeated in her contribution to (1981) 'Memorial Meeting for Dr Wilfred Bion', in *Int R.of Psycho-Anal.*, 8:3-14

[iii] For instance, Benjamin Libet's findings are reported by Ramachandran 2003 in the Reith Lectures, Radio 4 The Emerging Mind http://www.bbc.co.uk/radio4/reith2003

[iv] Freud, S. (1920) 'One of the Difficulties of Psycho-Analysis' *Int. J. Psycho-Anal. 1:17-23*

[v] Freud, S. (1916-17 [1915-17]) 'The Manifest Content of Dreams and the Latent Dream Thoughts', in *(1973) Introductory Lectures on Psychoanalysis,* Harmondsworth: Pelican

[vi] Many people have conceptualised working in this area and in different ways, including Bion's alpha function and beta elements, Kristeva's semiotic and Jo Klein's patients who are not ready for interpretation, to name but 3:
Bion, W.R. (1962) *Learning from Experience.* London: Heinemann
Klein, J. (1987) *Our Need for Others and its Roots in Infancy.* London: Tavistock
Kristeva, J. (1980) *Powers of Horror,* trans. L.S. Roudiez (1982), New York and Chichester: Columbia University Press

[vii] A more complete account of this work can be found in Jacobs, M.

(1998) 'Seeing and being seen in the experience of the client and the therapist' in the *European Journal of Psychotherapy, Counselling and Health, Vol 1 no 2 August 1998:213-230, pp223-4*

viii Freud, S. (1925[4]) as above

ix Hazel Muir's article, 'What Happens at Absolute Zero', 17.2.10 www.newscientist.com

x This is also the territory of prejudice and xenophobia – when we cannot incorporate something unfamiliar or someone apparently different from ourselves, the difference generates complexity and therefore anxiety. If we are unable to embrace this stimulus, unable to be interested but instead feel our cherished, established order is being threatened, then we reject the other as unacceptably different and thus make of them an enemy.

xi Williams, P. lecture, *The worm that flies in the night*, Los Angeles, March 11 2006

xii Marion Milner in conversation with Rita Simon and others, 1997

xiii Ogden, T. (1994) *Subjects of Analysis,* & (1999) *Reverie and Interpretation,* London: Karnac

xiv Freud, S.(1925[1924]) as above

xv Freud, S. (1915-16) 'The Manifest Content of Dreams and Latent Dream Thoughts' in *(1973) Introductory Lectures on Psychoanalysis*, Harmondsworth: Pelican, gives a lovely interpretation of a dream ostensibly about purchasing theatre tickets

[xvi] Bollas, c. (1987) *The Shadow of the Object: Psychoanalysis of the Unthought Known,* London: Free Association Books

[xvii] This does not mean that there should be no regulation of psychoanalytic practice, on the contrary. Free range chickens are subject to the farmer's husbandry – they do not roam wild. My concern is simply that the form of any regulation be suited to the practice rather than forcing it to become a different beast, thus driving it to extinction.

[xviii] Jacobs, L. (1973) *A Jewish theology.* Darton, Longman & Todd, p188

[xix] As an art therapist I didn't provide rulers or rubbers, on the basis that in emotional life there are no straight lines and we cannot erase what we don't like: we have to work with it and find a way to make it part of our creation.

[xx] Culbert-Koehn, J-A. (1997) 'Don't get stuck in the mother: Regression in analysis' in *Journal of Analytical Psychology 42:99-104*

[xxi] See http://www.thecapitalnews.co.uk/tsunami.htm

[xxii] Jacobs, L. (1973) p. 188 above

[xxiii] Again there are many different ways that the importance of a 'third' principle has been thought about, not least of all in the form of Freud's own Oedipus Complex. Melanie Klein thought the onset of the Oedipal situation was much earlier than Freud had, and she conceptualised it in terms of the infantile phantasy of the 'father's penis inside the mother'. Lacan used the idea of the 'nom(n) du pere' to evoke the paternal metaphor and authority of 'third-ness'. Freud, S. (1924) 'The dissolution of the Oedipus Complex', *SE XIX,*

(1961) London: Hogarth

Klein, M. (1928) 'Early stages of the Oedipus conflict' in (1975) *Love, Guilt and Reparation and Other Works 1921 – 1945,* London: Hogarth

Lacan, J. (1960) 'The subversion of the subject and the dialectic of desire in the Freudian unconscious', in *Ecrits: A selection,* trans. A Sheridan (1977), London: Tavistock

[xxiv] Jacobs, L. (1973) p. 188 as above

[xxv] Jacobs, L. (1973) p. 189 as above

[xxvi] Bion's 'O' and Nathan Field's 'four dimensionality' are interesting in relation to these (impossible) reaches:

Bion, W.R. (1965) *Transformations,* London: Heinemann and (1970) *Attention and Interpretation,* London: Tavistock

Field, N. (1996) *Breakdown and Breakthrough - psychotherapy in a new dimension,* London: Routledge

Also

Ann Brontë, 'On becoming'(1846)

> Oh dreadful is the check
> - intense the agony -
> When the ear begins to hear,
> And the eye begins to see;
> When the pulse begins to throb,
> And the brain to think again;
> The soul to feel the flesh ,
> And the flesh to feel the chain'.

Brontë, A. (1972) *Poems* (Denis Thompson, ed.) London: Chatto and Windus

[xxvii] White, J. (2006) *Generation.* Routledge: London

Bibliography

(Details of publications specifically referred to are provided in the notes & are not repeated here)

- Marie Cardinal (1975) *Les Mots pour le Dire,* eds. Grasset, translated into English (1984) *The Words to Say It,* Picador. While the translation is out of print it is possible to get second hand copies.
- George Eliot (1871-2) *Middlemarch,* (2003) London: Penguin Classics
- Moris Farhi (2009) *A Designated Man*, London: Telegram
- Maxim Gorky (1906) *Mother*, (2008) Bibliobazaar and others
- Naomi Klein (2007) *The Shock Doctrine,* London: Penguin
- JMG Le Clezio (1980) *Désert,* Folio and *Desert,* trans. C. Dickson (2010) Atlantic Books
- Owen Sheers (2007) *Resistance,* London: Faber

Films

- *Death and the Maiden* (2002) director Roman Polanski, Films Sans Frontiers, adapted from the play by Ariel Dorfman
- *The Company of Wolves* (1984) director Neil Jordan, ITV Studios Home Entertainment, from the short story by Angela Carter in (1998) *The Bloody Chamber,* Vintage Classics
- *The Lemon Tree (2009)* director Eran Riklis, Unanimous Pictures, from the book by Sandy Tolen (2008): Black Swan Books
- *Pan's Labyrinth* (2006) director and writer: Guillermo del Toro, Optimum Home Entertainment

Poems

- Constantine P. Cavafy (1911) *Ithaca*
- Rudyard Kipling (1910) *If-*
- Derek Walcott (2010) *White Egrets*, esp *The Acacia Trees*